Sanjeev Kapoor's

INTERNATIONAL CUISINE SERIES

THAI Cooking

Sanjeev Kapoor's

INTERNATIONAL CUISINE SERIES

THAI Cooking

In association with Alyona Kapoor

Popular Prakashan

www.popularprakashan.com

Published by
POPULAR PRAKASHAN PVT. LTD.
301, Mahalaxmi Chambers
22, Bhulabhai Desai Road
Mumbai - 400 026
for Khana Khazana Publications Pvt. Ltd.

First Published 2007
First Reprint August 2010

(4076)
ISBN: 978-81-7991-328-4

Photography: Bharat Bhirangi
Typeset by Manasi Parab

PRINTED IN INDIA
by G.H Prints Pvt. Ltd.
A-256, Okhla Industrial Area
Phase I, New Delhi - 1100 02

DEDICATION

To my readers and fellow-travellers on a gastronomical tour of the great cuisines of the world. May we continue to discover and experience together the unique flavours of many lands.

AUTHOR'S NOTE

Creamy coconut curries redolent with the fragrances of the Orient; cool, crunchy salads, spiked with fiery chillies; smoky stir-fries cloaked in hot and sweet sauces. Thai food has found a permanent place on the Indian palate and plate.

When one thinks of Thai cuisine, one pictures a banquet of exotic dishes with beautifully carved fruit and vegetables adorning the table. The reality is, however, that in Thailand, a meal comprises a bowl of steaming glutinous rice with a portion of meat, fish or vegetable, and one or two of a variety of spicy sauces on the side. Aficionados of Thai cuisine will know that the array of exotic dishes featured on restaurant menus represents the culinary diversity of Thai regional food.

Som Tam, the popular papaya salad sprinkled with crunchy peanuts, is a typical dish from the Northeast, the poorest region of Thailand. Fish sauce, an essential ingredient in Thai food, is produced in the South and Gulf coastal region, which is also home to the rich coconut curries, seafood dishes and the spicy Massaman curry contributed by Indian Muslim immigrants to Thai cuisine.

The heady jasmine-scented rice which is unique to Thailand, is a product of the Central Plains, also known as the rice bowl of the country. Rice noodles such as Pad Thai are a natural by-product, the noodles denoting the strong Chinese influence on Thai cooking. The Central Plains are also the home of Tom Yum, the popular Hot and Sour Soup and everyone's favourite Green Curry. Bangkok is the street food capital of the country with its rows of food stalls selling an array of snacks including barbecued meats, fish cakes and spring rolls. And finally, the intricately carved vegetables and fruit, which one associates with Thai cuisine, are an example of what is called Palace Food, a reference no doubt to the royal repasts of the rulers of the kingdom of Siam.

Thai cooking, like Chinese cooking, from which it derives many of its culinary styles, lays a great deal of emphasis on the freshness of ingredients, the harmonious blend of flavours and textures, which engage all the senses at the same time. Every dish is an aromatic mélange of four flavours: salty, sweet, sour and piquant. Galangal (similar to ginger), kaffir lime leaves, basil and lemon grass provide the aromas; Nam Pla or fish sauce and dried shrimp paste contribute the salty flavours; sweet notes are sounded by palm sugar (brown sugar is a good alternative) and coconut; while tamarind and the juice of the kaffir lime add that touch of sourness which appears to complete the bouquet of tastes. And just when one is beguiled by the smooth harmony of flavours, the searing heat of the red hot bird's eye chilli, intrudes on the senses and leaves a lingering fire on the tongue. Which is why, I am sure, Thai meals end with the soothing, creamy balm of tropical fruit purées and coconut milk desserts!

I hope you enjoy this banquet I have laid out especially for you, so you can experience the flavours of Thailand in your own home.

Happy Cooking!

ACKNOWLEDGEMENTS

Afsheen Panjwani
Anand Bhandiwad
Anil Bhandari
Anupa Das
Bharati Anand
Bhartendu Sharma
Drs. Meena & Ram Prabhoo
Gajendra Mule
Ganesh Pednekar
Harpal Singh Sokhi
Jayadeep Chaubal
Jyotsna & Mayur Dvivedi
Lohana Khaandaan
Mahendra Ghanekar
Manasi Morajkar
Mrs. Lata Lohana & Capt. K. K. Lohana
Namrata & Sanjiv Bahl
Neelima Acharya
Neena Murdeshwar
Pooja & Rajeev Kapoor
Rajeev Matta
Rita D'Souza
Rutika Samtani
Saurabh Mishra
Smeeta Bhatkal
Tripta Bhagattjee
Trupti Kale
Vaishali Parekh
Vinayak Gawande

CONTENTS

RICE AND NOODLES

DESSERTS

CURRY PASTES

CHIANG MAI NOODLE SOUP

Ingredients

200 grams boneless chicken, cut into thin strips

200 grams egg noodles, blanched

1 tablespoon oil

1 tablespoon Red Curry Paste (*page 103*)

¼ teaspoon turmeric powder

4 cups Chicken Stock (*page 22*)

1 tablespoon fish sauce

18-20 black peppercorns, ground

salt to taste

½ cup Coconut Milk (*page 68*)

1 tablespoon lemon juice

Method

1 Heat the oil in a wok; add the chicken strips and sauté for five minutes.

2 Add the red curry paste and turmeric powder and sauté for another two minutes.

3. Add the chicken stock, fish sauce, ground peppercorns and salt and simmer for ten minutes, or until the chicken is cooked.
4. Stir in the coconut milk. Add the blanched noodles and remove from heat. Stir in the lemon juice and serve hot.

CHEF'S TIP

To blanch noodles, cook in boiling salted water till *al dente* (cooked, but still firm to the bite). Drain, refresh in cold water and drain again.

MUSHROOM SOUP WITH CHILLIES

Ingredients

20-25 fresh button mushrooms, quartered

4 cups Vegetable Stock (*see below*)

1 tablespoon oil

salt to taste

1 inch ginger, cut into strips

¼ cup chopped fresh coriander leaves

4-5 stalks spring onion greens, chopped

Chilli Paste

1 tablespoon oil

4 dried red chillies, halved

4 shallots, chopped

3 garlic cloves, chopped

1 inch galangal, sliced

Method

1 For the chilli paste, heat the oil in a pan; add the dried chillies, shallots, garlic and galangal and sauté for four to five minutes. Cool and grind to a fine paste.

2 For the soup, heat one tablespoon of oil in a separate pan; add the mushrooms and sauté for one minute. Transfer the mushrooms to a plate.

3 To the same pan, add the vegetable stock and bring to a boil.

4 Add the salt, sautéed mushrooms and ginger strips. Stir in the chilli paste and simmer for five minutes.

5 Sprinkle coriander leaves and spring onion greens over the soup and serve hot.

VEGETABLE STOCK

Place 1 sliced onion, 1 sliced carrot, a 2-3 inch piece of celery, 2 garlic cloves, 1 bay leaf, 5-6 black peppercorns and 2-3 cloves in a pan with 5 cups of water and bring to a boil. Simmer for 15 minutes and strain.

CHICKEN AND GALANGAL SOUP

Ingredients

100 grams boneless chicken breast, cut into strips

2 tablespoons oil

salt to taste

2 cups Chicken Stock (*page 22*)

1 cup Coconut Milk (*page 68*)

1 teaspoon brown sugar

2-3 bird's eye chillies, slit

3 kaffir lime leaves

10-12 oyster mushrooms, halved

2 tablespoons fish sauce

1 tablespoon lemon juice

1 tablespoon chopped fresh coriander leaves

Spice Paste

1 tablespoon oil

2 inches galangal, sliced

2 tablespoons chopped lemon grass

2 coriander roots, chopped

3 shallots, chopped

4-5 garlic cloves

5 white peppercorns

Method

1 For the spice paste, heat one tablespoon of oil in a pan; add the galangal, lemon grass, coriander roots, shallots, garlic and white peppercorns and sauté for four to five minutes. Cool and grind to a fine paste.

2 Add two tablespoons of oil to the same pan; add the chicken and salt and cook for five minutes. Remove the chicken from the pan and set aside.

3 To the same pan, add the chicken stock and coconut milk and bring to a boil.

4 Add the brown sugar, chillies, lime leaves and oyster mushrooms and simmer for ten minutes.

5 Stir in the spice paste and sautéed chicken and simmer for another ten minutes.

6 Season the soup with fish sauce, lemon juice and salt.

7 Garnish with chopped coriander leaves and serve hot.

CHEF'S TIP

If bird's eye chillies are not available, use fresh red chillies.

SPICY CHICKEN AND COCONUT SOUP

Ingredients

½ cup boneless chicken strips

1½ cups tender coconut water

½ cup tender coconut flesh, chopped

2-3 green chillies, halved

3 cups Chicken Stock (*see below*)

5 large oyster mushrooms, roughly torn

4 kaffir lime leaves

salt to taste

1 tablespoon fish sauce

a pinch of sugar

2 tablespoons lemon juice

2 tablespoons chopped fresh coriander leaves

Method

1 In a non-stick pan, roast the coconut flesh with green chillies until brown.

2 Bring the chicken stock to a boil in a large pan; add the chicken, coconut water, roasted coconut and chillies, oyster mushrooms, lime leaves and salt. Bring once again to a boil.

3 Lower heat and simmer until the chicken is tender. Stir in the fish sauce, sugar and lemon juice.

4 Serve hot, garnished with coriander leaves.

CHICKEN STOCK

Boil 200 grams chicken bones in water for 5 minutes. Drain and discard water. Boil blanched bones with a roughly chopped carrot, celery stalk, leek, 2-3 parsley stalks, 6-7 black peppercorns, 5-6 cloves, 1 bay leaf and 10 cups of water. Remove any scum which rises to the surface and replace it with more cold water. Simmer for at least 1 hour. Remove from heat, strain, cool and store in a refrigerator till further use.

MIXED VEGETABLE SOUP

Ingredients

¼ medium Chinese cabbage, shredded

¼ small cauliflower, coarsely chopped

4 one-inch celery pieces, chopped

100 grams tofu (bean curd), cut into ½-inch cubes

2 tablespoons oil

2 garlic cloves, crushed

1 fresh red chilli, sliced

5-6 cups Vegetable Stock (*page 17*)

salt to taste

¼ teaspoon white pepper powder

1 teaspoon brown sugar

1 tablespoon light soy sauce

2 tablespoons chopped fresh coriander leaves

Method

1 Heat the oil in a wok; add the garlic and fresh red chilli and sauté for half a minute.

2 Add the cabbage, cauliflower and celery and sauté for another minute.

3 Add the vegetable stock and bring to a boil. Lower heat, add the salt, pepper powder, brown sugar and soy sauce and simmer for five or six minutes, or until the vegetables are tender. Add the tofu and coriander leaves and serve hot.

TOM YUM KUNG

Hot and Sour Prawn Soup

Ingredients

20-30 (200 grams) small prawns

2 lemon grass stalks

6 kaffir lime leaves

4 fresh green or red chillies

salt to taste

5-6 fresh button mushrooms, sliced

2 tablespoons fish sauce

1 teaspoon Red Curry Paste (*page 103*)

2-3 tablespoons lemon juice

2 tablespoons fresh coriander leaves, chopped

Method

1 Remove the heads and shells of the prawns and reserve. Devein and wash the prawns thoroughly under running water.

2 Wash the prawn heads and shells and put into a pan with four to five cups of water. Crush the lemon grass stems, two lime leaves and two chillies with a mortar and pestle and add to the pan. Finely chop the remaining chillies.

3 Bring the mixture to a boil and add salt to taste. Lower heat, cover and simmer for fifteen minutes. Remove from heat and strain the stock.

4 Bring the strained stock to a boil in a large pan. Add the mushrooms and prawns and simmer for two to three minutes, or until the prawns are cooked and pink.

5 Stir in the fish sauce, red curry paste and lemon juice. Adjust the seasoning.

6 Pour into a serving bowl and garnish with the coriander leaves and the remaining chillies and lime leaves. Serve piping hot.

CHEF'S TIP

To devein prawns, using a thin, sharp knife, make a shallow cut along one side of the dark thin vein that runs down the back of the prawn. Run the tip of the knife down the length of the vein to remove it.

MARINATED PRAWN SALAD

Ingredients

15 (200 grams) medium prawns, peeled, deveined and blanched

1 cup grated fresh coconut

4 shallots, sliced

2 lemon grass stalks, chopped

3 kaffir lime leaves, finely shredded

a few fresh mint leaves, to garnish

Dressing

a pinch of brown sugar

4 tablespoons lemon juice

1 tablespoon fish sauce

2 fresh red chillies, chopped

1 garlic clove, chopped

salt to taste

Method

1. In a large bowl, toss together the prawns, coconut, shallots, lemon grass and lime leaves.
2. For the dressing, mix together the brown sugar, lemon juice, fish sauce, red chillies, garlic and salt in a small bowl.
3. Pour the dressing over the prawn and coconut mixture and toss gently to mix. Serve, garnished with fresh mint leaves.

BEAN SPROUT SALAD

Ingredients

2 cups bean sprouts

4 tablespoons chopped tender coconut flesh

2 tablespoons vinegar

2 medium onions, sliced

1 tablespoon chopped coriander leaves

Spice Paste

3 tablespoons grated fresh coconut, roasted

3 tablespoons roasted peanuts, skinned

a large pinch of salt

Method

1 For the spice paste, pound the ingredients together with a mortar and pestle till smooth.

2 Mix the paste with the bean sprouts and tender coconut. Add the vinegar and toss to mix.

3 Serve, sprinkled generously with onions and coriander leaves.

GRILLED CHICKEN SALAD

Ingredients

2 (150 grams each) boneless chicken breasts

Garlic Oil, for basting (*see below*)

1 head of lettuce

5 spring onions, chopped

½ cucumber, cut into ½-inch pieces

8-10 fresh button mushrooms, thinly sliced

Dressing

3 tablespoons fish sauce

4 tablespoons lemon juice

1 garlic clove, crushed

2 teaspoons brown sugar

2 fresh red chillies, seeded and cut into thin strips

salt to taste

Garnish

1 tablespoon chopped fresh coriander leaves

2 green chillies, sliced

Method

1. Preheat the grill. Place the chicken breasts on the grill pan and brush liberally with garlic oil. Grill until cooked through and golden brown, turning once, to brown both sides evenly. Set aside to cool.
2. For the dressing, put the fish sauce, lemon juice, garlic, brown sugar and one fresh red chilli into a small saucepan. Cook over low heat, stirring continuously, till the sugar dissolves. Adjust salt and remove from heat.
3. Arrange the lettuce leaves in a serving dish and sprinkle with spring onions, cucumber and mushrooms.
4. Cut the grilled chicken into strips and arrange on top of the vegetables. Pour the warm dressing over and garnish with the coriander leaves, green chillies and remaining fresh red chilli.
5. Serve warm.

GARLIC OIL

Heat 4 tablespoons oil in a small frying pan and add 6 to 8 crushed garlic cloves. Cook over low heat, stirring occasionally, until the garlic is golden. Store and use as required.

GREEN PAPAYA SALAD

Som Tam

Ingredients

2 cups shredded green, unripe papaya
4 garlic cloves
salt to taste
1 fresh red chilli, roughly chopped
4 cherry tomatoes, quartered
2 tablespoons lemon juice
2 tablespoons brown sugar
1 tablespoon fish sauce
½ tablespoon tamarind pulp
½ cup roasted peanuts, crushed

Method

1. Place the shredded papaya in a large bowl and crush lightly with a pestle.
2. Crush the garlic cloves and salt with a mortar and pestle. Add the red chilli and cherry tomatoes and continue to crush lightly.
3. Add the crushed garlic mixture to the papaya with the lemon juice and mix well.

4 Crush the brown sugar, fish sauce and tamarind pulp with the mortar and pestle. Add to the papaya mixture and mix.

5 Add the crushed roasted peanuts and toss to mix.

6 Serve immediately.

CHEF'S TIP

You can use jaggery instead of brown sugar, and soy sauce in place of fish sauce.

FRIED GOLDEN BAGS

Ingredients

20 (four inch x four inch) wonton wrappers

20 thin stalks spring onion greens

oil for deep-frying

Stuffing

½ cup shredded raw crab meat

5-6 medium prawns, peeled, deveined and chopped

5-6 garlic cloves, chopped

1 tablespoon chopped fresh coriander leaves

5-6 black peppercorns, crushed

salt to taste

1 spring onion, chopped

½ green chilli, chopped

½ tablespoon dark soy sauce

½ tablespoon fish sauce

Method

1. Mix together all the ingredients for the stuffing in a bowl.
2. Spread out the wonton squares on a flat surface; place equal quantities of the crab meat stuffing in the centre of each wonton.
3. Pull the four corners up into the middle to make little bags.
4. Secure the bags around the middle with the spring onion greens. Be careful that the greens do not break while tying.
5. Heat the oil in a wok. Deep-fry the wonton bags till golden brown and crisp. Drain on absorbent paper.
6. Serve hot with chilli sauce.

CHEF'S TIP

Dip the spring onion greens in warm water to make them more pliable.

CHICKEN AND PRAWN DUMPLINGS

Ingredients

16 (four inch x four inch) wonton wrappers

300 grams chicken mince (*keema*)

8 prawns, deveined and halved lengthways

1 egg

4-5 garlic cloves, chopped

1 tablespoon chopped fresh coriander leaves

10-12 black peppercorns, crushed

salt to taste

½ tablespoon fish sauce

½ tablespoon soy sauce

Dipping Sauce

4 tablespoons light soy sauce

4 tablespoons tomato ketchup

1 tablespoon Garlic Oil (page 30)

salt to taste

Method

1. To make the filling, process the chicken mince, egg, garlic, coriander leaves, peppercorns, salt, fish sauce and soy sauce in a food processor.
2. Cut half an inch off the corners of each wonton wrapper to make an octagonal shape.
3. Place a teaspoon of the chicken filling in the centre of each wrapper and bring up the edges to form a cup.
4. Pinch the side of the wonton 'cup' between your forefinger and thumb to form pleats. Tuck half a prawn into each wonton dumpling.
5. Arrange the dumplings in two greased steamers and steam for fifteen minutes.
6. To make the dipping sauce, mix together the soy sauce, tomato ketchup, garlic oil and salt in a small bowl.
7. Serve the dumplings with the dipping sauce.

SPICY FISH CAKES

Ingredients

400 grams fish fillets, skinned and cut into chunks

3 tablespoons Red Curry Paste (*page 103*)

2 tablespoons fish sauce

2 tablespoons rice flour

salt to taste

8 kaffir lime leaves, finely shredded

oil for deep-frying

Method

1 Process the fish chunks and red curry paste in a food processor or blender to a paste. Alternatively, pound the fish and red curry paste with a mortar and pestle.

2 Transfer the mixture to a bowl; add the fish sauce, rice flour and salt and knead into a stiff dough. Add the lime leaves and knead again.

3 Divide into eight portions and shape into balls. Flatten each ball with moistened hands into a half-inch thick round cake.

4 Heat the oil in a wok; fry the fish cakes, a few at a time, for four to five minutes on each side, or until cooked and golden. Do not over-fry them.

5 Drain on absorbent paper and serve hot with chilli sauce.

EGG NETS

Ingredients

6 eggs, chilled

2 tablespoons oil + for deep-frying

6 coriander roots

a pinch of salt

8 garlic cloves

20 white peppercorns

½ cup minced, peeled and deveined shrimps (small prawns)

4 tablespoons fish sauce

6 tablespoons sugar

2 tablespoons finely chopped lemon grass

6 medium onions, sliced

2 fresh red chillies, cut into strips

6 tablespoons chopped coriander leaves

Method

1 Whisk the chilled eggs lightly in a clean, dry glass or plastic container.

2 Heat a non-stick wok and grease it lightly. Dip your fingers into the egg mixture and wave them rapidly across the wok, so that the egg drizzles onto the wok. Move your hand backwards and forwards, and from side to side, to form a net pattern. It will be necessary to dip your hand into the egg mixture once or twice to make enough strands.

3 Circle the edges of the net with more egg mixture to form a border.

4 Remove the net gently and place it on absorbent paper. Repeat the process until all the mixture is used up. The nets can be made several hours in advance.

5 Pound the coriander roots, salt, garlic and peppercorns to a paste with a mortar and pestle.

6 Heat two tablespoons of oil in a pan and fry the paste till fragrant and golden. Add the minced shrimps and season with fish sauce and sugar. Sauté for one minute and remove from heat. Cool completely and add the lemon grass, onions, red chillies and coriander leaves.

7 Lay each net out on a board; spread some shrimp filling on the lower third of the net and roll the net up, gathering the ends in to make a cigar-shaped roll.

8 Cut into slices with a sharp knife and serve.

CHEF'S TIP

Do not over-beat the eggs as this will incorporate too much air, which will cause the eggs to bubble slightly and toughen on cooking.

FIRECRACKERS

Ingredients

16 (470 grams) jumbo prawns, peeled and deveined, with tails intact

1 teaspoon Red Curry Paste (*page 103*)

1 tablespoon fish sauce

salt to taste

16 (four-inch x four inch) wonton wrappers

16 egg noodles, soaked in boiling water for 2-3 minutes

oil for deep-frying

Method

1 Place the prawns on their sides and cut two slits through the underbelly of each prawn: the first slit about half an inch from the head, and the other about half an inch from the first slit. This will prevent the prawns from curling while cooking.

2 Mix together the red curry paste, fish sauce and salt in a shallow dish.

3 Add the prawns and mix well to coat with the paste. Cover and leave to marinate for ten minutes.

4. Place each wonton wrapper on a work surface at an angle, so that it forms a diamond; fold the top corner over so that the point is in the centre.
5. Place a prawn, slit side down, on the wrapper, with the tail projecting from the folded end. Fold the bottom corner over the other end of the prawn.
6. Fold the remaining sides of the wrapper over to make a tight roll. Tie a noodle around the roll in a bow.
7. Heat the oil in a wok and deep-fry the prawns till golden brown and cooked through. Drain on absorbent paper.
8. Serve hot.

CORN FRITTERS

Ingredients

1½ cups sweet corn kernels

6-8 garlic cloves, crushed

3 tablespoons chopped fresh coriander leaves

3 fresh red chillies, chopped

2-3 spring onions, chopped

1 tablespoon light soy sauce

¾ cup rice flour

2 eggs, lightly beaten

¼ teaspoon black pepper powder

salt to taste

oil for shallow-frying

Method

1 Place the sweet corn in a large bowl; add the garlic, coriander leaves, red chillies, spring onions, soy sauce, rice flour, eggs, pepper powder, salt and four tablespoons of water and mix well. The mixture should be firm enough to hold its shape, but not stiff.

2 Heat the oil in a frying pan; add spoonfuls of the corn mixture, gently spreading each dollop with the back of the spoon to make a round fritter.

3 Fry for one or two minutes on each side. Drain on absorbent paper. Serve hot with sweet chilli sauce.

THAI-STYLE BARBECUED VEGETABLES

Ingredients

8 small onions
4 zucchinis
1 red capsicum
1 yellow capsicum
1 green capsicum
8 fresh button mushrooms
1 medium carrot

Marinade

7-8 garlic cloves, chopped
salt to taste
3 teaspoons light soy sauce
2 tablespoons lemon juice
½ cup chopped fresh coriander leaves

Method

1. Chop all the vegetables into one-and-a-half inch chunks.
2. Mix together all the ingredients for the marinade.
3. Mix the marinade into the vegetables and leave to marinate for at least thirty minutes.
4. Thread the vegetables onto skewers and cook over a barbecue or grill, turning at regular intervals, till nicely browned. Serve hot.

Thai-Style Barbecued Vegetables

PUMPKIN CURRY

Ingredients

500 grams pumpkin, cut into ½-inch cubes
1 small sweet potato, cut into ½-inch cubes
2 medium carrots, thickly sliced
1 yellow capsicum, cut into ½-inch pieces
250 grams cherry tomatoes
1 cup boiled chickpeas, drained
2 tablespoons grated orange rind
salt to taste
a few basil leaves

Curry
4 garlic cloves
2 fresh red chillies
2 cups Coconut Milk (*page 68*)
1 teaspoon tamarind pulp
2 tablespoons light soy sauce
2 teaspoons brown sugar
2 teaspoons lemon juice
3 tablespoons orange juice
½ teaspoon turmeric powder
1 tablespoon rice vinegar
1 tablespoon coriander powder
1 tablespoon roasted cumin powder
1 teaspoon fennel (*saunf*) powder
1 large onion, sliced

Method

1 Grind all the ingredients for the curry to a smooth paste.

2 Pour the curry into a large wok and add the pumpkin, sweet potato and carrots. Cook over medium heat, stirring occasionally.

3 When the mixture comes to a boil, lower heat and simmer for six to eight minutes, or until the vegetables soften.

4 Add the capsicum, cherry tomatoes, chickpeas and orange rind. Stir well and simmer for another two minutes. Add salt to taste.

5 Serve hot, garnished with basil leaves.

MASSAMAN TOFU CURRY

Ingredients

400 grams tofu (bean curd), cubed

3 tablespoons Massaman Curry Paste (*page 101*)

1 tablespoon oil

1 tablespoon soy sauce

1 tablespoon lemon juice

2 tablespoons roasted peanuts

salt to taste

Method

1 Heat the oil in a pan; add the tofu and sauté for a few minutes.

2 Stir in the soy sauce, lemon juice and roasted peanuts.

3 Add the curry paste and salt to taste and mix well.

4 Cook for another fifteen minutes and serve hot.

STIR-FRIED EGGPLANT

Ingredients

1 large eggplant (brinjal), cubed

1 tablespoon fish sauce

2 tablespoons oyster sauce

1 teaspoon brown sugar

3 tablespoons oil

1 medium onion, chopped

6 garlic cloves, crushed

3 fresh red chillies, chopped

2 tablespoons light soy sauce

salt to taste

½ cup shredded basil leaves

Method

1 Mix the fish sauce with the oyster sauce and brown sugar.

2 Heat the oil in a wok; add the onion, half the garlic, the red chillies and eggplant cubes and stir-fry for five minutes. If necessary, sprinkle some water from time to time to prevent the ingredients from scorching.

3 Add the soy sauce and continue to stir-fry for five more minutes, or until the eggplant softens. Add the remaining garlic, the sauce mixture and a quarter cup of water.

4 Stir, and cook for two minutes, or till the sauce thickens. Add salt to taste and remove from heat.

5 Add three-fourth of the basil leaves and stir lightly.

6 Transfer to a platter and serve, garnished with the remaining basil.

VEGETABLES IN SWEET AND SOUR SAUCE

Ingredients

6 French beans, cut into 1-inch pieces

¼ medium cauliflower, separated into 1-inch florets

1 large carrot, cut into 1-inch pieces

1 large green capsicum, cut into 1-inch pieces

4 fresh button mushrooms, halved

1 large onion, cut into 1-inch pieces

Sauce

2 tablespoons cornflour

2 spring onions with greens

1½ tablespoons oil

¾ teaspoon ginger paste

¾ teaspoon garlic paste (optional)

½ teaspoon white pepper powder

a pinch of MSG (optional)

salt to taste

¾ cup Vegetable Stock (*page 17*)

½ cup tomato ketchup

1 tablespoon light soy sauce

2 tablespoons sugar

1½ teaspoons vinegar

Method

1 Place the French beans, cauliflower and carrot in a pan with one cup of water. Bring to a boil and cook for five to six minutes. Drain.

2 For the sauce, mix the cornflour with three tablespoons of water. Cut the spring onion bulbs into thin slices and finely chop the greens. Reserve the greens for garnishing.

3 Heat the oil in a wok; gently stir-fry the ginger paste, garlic paste and spring onions. Add the white pepper powder, MSG and salt and mix well.

4 Stir in the vegetable stock, tomato ketchup, soy sauce, sugar and vinegar. Cook over medium heat for four to five minutes. Add the French beans, cauliflower, carrot, capsicum, mushrooms and onion and mix well.

5 Cook over high heat for six or seven minutes. Stir in the cornflour mixture and cook for another seven or eight minutes.

6 Garnish with spring onion greens and serve immediately.

CHICKEN WITH CHILLI JAM

Ingredients

3 (150 grams each) boneless chicken breasts, cut into strips

2 teaspoons oil

4 shallots, chopped

½ head of broccoli, cut into small florets

12 snow peas, halved

¼ cup roasted cashew nuts

2 tablespoons light soy sauce

salt to taste

white pepper powder to taste

Chilli Jam

2 teaspoons oil

4 fresh red chillies, sliced

1½ inches ginger, shredded

⅓ cup sugar

2 tablespoons lemon juice

Method

1 To make the chilli jam, heat the oil in a wok over medium heat; add the red chillies and ginger and stir-fry for one minute.

2 Add the sugar, lemon juice and one-third cup of water. Cook, stirring continuously, for three minutes, or till thick. Remove from heat and keep warm.

3 For the chicken, heat the oil in a separate wok; add the chicken and shallots and stir-fry for three minutes, or until chicken is lightly browned.

4 Add the broccoli, snow peas, cashew nuts, soy sauce, salt and white pepper powder and stir-fry for three minutes, or until the vegetables change colour.

5 Place the chicken on a serving plate, top with the chilli jam and serve immediately.

CHEF'S TIP

You can also serve hot and tangy Chilli Jam with grilled fish and prawns.

CHICKEN IN GREEN CURRY

Ingredients

200 grams boneless chicken breasts, cubed

1½ tablespoons Green Curry Paste (*page 102*)

½ tablespoon oil

1 medium onion, chopped

8-10 basil leaves, shredded

3 kaffir lime leaves, shredded

1¼ cups Coconut Milk (*page 68*)

1 tablespoon fish sauce

salt to taste

Method

1 Heat the oil in a wok or a pan; add the onion and sauté till golden. Stir in the green curry paste and cook for two minutes till fragrant.

2 Add the chicken, three-fourth of the basil leaves, the lime leaves, coconut milk and fish sauce.

3 Bring the mixture to a boil, lower heat and simmer for twelve to fifteen minutes, or until the chicken is tender and the sauce is thick. Add salt to taste.

4 Serve hot, garnished with the remaining basil leaves.

BARBEQUED CHICKEN

Ingredients

2 (150 grams each) boneless chicken breasts
2 dried red chillies
1 garlic clove
3 small onions, chopped
1 teaspoon brown sugar
¼ cup thick Coconut Milk (*page 68*)
1 teaspoon fish sauce
½ tablespoon tamarind pulp
salt to taste
2 tablespoons oil
4-5 basil leaves

Method

1 Make four incisions on each chicken breast with a sharp knife.
2 Grind the red chillies, garlic and onions with a little water to a fine paste.
3 Transfer the paste to a bowl, add the brown sugar, thick coconut milk , fish sauce, tamarind pulp and salt and mix well.
4 Marinate the chicken breasts in the paste for one hour, preferably in a refrigerator.
5 Preheat the grill or barbecue. Place the chicken breasts on a piece of foil and grill for about four minutes on each side, brushing occasionally with oil, until cooked through. Serve hot, garnished with basil leaves.

CHICKEN IN RED CURRY

Ingredients

200 grams boneless chicken breasts, cubed

¾ tablespoon Red Curry Paste (*page 103*)

1 cup Coconut Milk (*page 68*)

½ tablespoon light soy sauce

½ teaspoon brown sugar

½ tablespoon lemon juice

6-8 basil leaves, shredded

1 teaspoon olive oil

salt to taste

¼ teaspoon black pepper powder

¼ medium green capsicum, cut into strips

½ medium carrot, shredded

½ medium zucchini, shredded

½ cup Chicken Stock (*page 22*)

Method

1 For the red curry, combine the red curry and coconut milk paste in a pan. Bring to a boil, lower heat and simmer for five minutes. Add the soy sauce, brown sugar and lemon juice. Stir and simmer for five more minutes. Add the basil leaves and remove from heat.

2 Heat the olive oil in a large non-stick pan; add the chicken cubes and season with salt and pepper. Sauté the chicken over medium heat for about eight to ten minutes.

3 Add the capsicum, carrot and zucchini; sauté until the vegetables are cooked.

4 Add the red curry and chicken stock and simmer for five minutes.

5 Serve hot with steamed rice.

BRAISED LAMB WITH SPINACH AND LEEKS

Ingredients

400 grams boneless lamb, cut into ½-inch thick slices

20 spinach leaves, stems removed

1 medium leek, sliced

2 tablespoons light soy sauce

2 tablespoons fish sauce

3 tablespoons oil

½ cup chopped fresh coriander leaves

15-20 black peppercorns, crushed

2 garlic cloves, crushed

1 tablespoon brown sugar

salt to taste

3 tablespoons lemon juice

Method

1 Place the lamb slices in a bowl; add the soy sauce, fish sauce, one tablespoon of oil, coriander leaves, crushed peppercorns, garlic, brown sugar and salt. Mix well and marinate the lamb for one hour in a refrigerator.

2. Drain the lamb and reserve the marinade.
3. Heat one tablespoon of oil in a wok; add the lamb slices and stir-fry for five minutes.
4. Add one cup of water and cover the wok with a lid. Cook the lamb over high heat till dry. Remove the lamb slices from the wok and keep warm.
5. Heat the remaining oil in the same wok; add the leek and stir-fry for two minutes.
6. Add the spinach leaves and cook for another thirty seconds. Add the leftover marinade and half a cup of water.
7. Bring to a boil, lower heat and simmer for five minutes; adjust seasoning.
8. Pour the sauce over the lamb, drizzle with lemon juice and serve immediately.

MASSAMAN MUTTON CURRY

Ingredients

500 grams boneless lamb, cubed

Massaman Curry Paste (*page 101*)

½ cup thick Coconut Milk (*see below*)

2 cups thin Coconut Milk (*see below*)

¼ teaspoon green cardamom powder

3 one-inch cinnamon sticks

3 large potatoes, cubed

1 tablespoon roasted peanuts, crushed

10 stalks spring onion greens, chopped

3 bay leaves

1½ tablespoons brown sugar

3 tablespoons fish sauce

3 tablespoons tamarind pulp

salt to taste

Method

1. Combine the curry paste with thick coconut milk in a pan and cook over low heat for five minutes.
2. Add the lamb cubes and continue to cook for eight to ten minutes. Add the thin coconut milk, bring to a boil, lower heat and simmer gently for ten minutes.

3 Add the green cardamom powder, cinnamon, potato cubes, crushed peanuts, spring onion greens, bay leaves, brown sugar, fish sauce, tamarind pulp and salt to taste.

4 Bring to a boil, lower heat and simmer till the lamb and potatoes are cooked.

5 Serve hot with rice.

COCONUT MILK

To extract 1 cup thick coconut milk, process 1 cup of fresh grated coconut with ½ a cup of warm water in blender. Pass through a fine strainer or piece of muslin. For thin coconut milk process the coconut once more with 1 cup of warm water. Strain. You can also use the ready-made packaged coconut milk.

DEEP-FRIED CHILLI FISH

Ingredients

1 whole (1 kilogram) fish such as Pomfret, cleaned
4 fresh red chillies, chopped
4 coriander roots
3 garlic cloves, crushed
6-7 black peppercorns, crushed
salt to taste
oil for deep-frying

Red Chilli Sauce
$^{2}/_{3}$ cup sugar
8 fresh red chillies, sliced
4 medium onions, sliced
$^{1}/_{3}$ cup vinegar
salt to taste

Method

1 Make diagonal slits on both sides of the fish.

2 Grind the fresh red chillies, coriander roots, garlic, peppercorns and salt to a paste.

3 Spread the paste on both sides of the fish and marinate for thirty minutes.

4 To make the red chilli sauce, place the sugar, red chillies, onions, vinegar, salt and one-third cup of water in a pan; cook over low heat, stirring continuously, till the sugar dissolves completely and the sauce thickens. Keep warm.

5 Heat the oil in a large wok. Deep-fry the fish till crisp on both sides. Drain on absorbent paper.

6 Serve hot with the red chilli sauce.

CHEF'S TIP

Coriander roots are widely used in Thai cooking. Scrape off the outer layer of thick roots before using.

PRAWNS IN COCONUT SAUCE

Ingredients

20 (300 grams) medium prawns, peeled and deveined
1 cup Coconut Milk (*page 68*)
2 fresh red chillies, seeded and chopped
1 medium onion, chopped
1 lemon grass stalk, chopped
1 inch galangal, chopped
1 teaspoon turmeric powder
8 basil leaves
2 teaspoons lemon juice
1 teaspoon fish sauce
salt to taste
1 spring onion green, cut into strips

Method

1. Grind the red chillies, onion, lemon grass and galangal to a paste. Cook the paste in a wok, stirring continuously, for two to three minutes.
2. Stir in the turmeric powder and half a cup of water. Bring the mixture to a boil, lower heat and simmer for three or four minutes, or until most of the water evaporates.
3. Stir in the coconut milk and prawns and simmer, stirring occasionally, for about four minutes, or until the prawns are just firm and pink. Stir in the basil leaves, lemon juice, fish sauce and salt. Serve hot, garnished with spring onion greens.

HOT AND FRAGRANT FISH

Ingredients

2 whole (450 grams) trouts

4 large green chillies, seeded and chopped

10 shallots

10 garlic cloves

4 tablespoons lemon juice

3 tablespoons fish sauce

2 tablespoons brown sugar

8 kaffir lime leaves, finely shredded

salt to taste

1 tablespoon oil

2 stalks spring onion greens, chopped

Method

1. Clean the fish well and make a few slits on both sides.
2. Wrap the chillies, shallots and garlic in aluminium foil and place under a hot grill for ten minutes.
3. When the package is cool enough to handle, pound the contents with a mortar and pestle, or grind coarsely in a food processor.

4 Add the lemon juice, fish sauce, brown sugar, lime leaves, salt and oil; mix well.

5 Stuff the paste into the slits in the fish. Smear a little paste on the skin as well.

6 Grill the fish for about five minutes on each side, until just cooked through.

7 Place the grilled fish on a platter, garnish with spring onion greens and serve hot with steamed rice.

CHEF'S TIP

If trouts are not available, use any other firm fish such as pomfrets.

FRIED JASMINE RICE WITH BASIL

Ingredients

4 cups cooked Jasmine rice

15-20 basil leaves, roughly chopped

3 tablespoons oil

1 medium onion, chopped

7-8 garlic cloves, chopped

1 tablespoon Red Curry Paste (*page 103*)

¼ cup shelled green peas, blanched

½ head of broccoli, separated into small florets, blanched

1 large carrot, diced and blanched

salt to taste

white pepper powder to taste

2 stalks spring onions greens, chopped

Method

1 Heat two tablespoons of oil in a wok; add the onion and garlic and sauté for two or three minutes.

2 Add the red curry paste, mix well and sauté for two minutes.

3 Add the rice, green peas, broccoli, carrot, salt, white pepper powder and toss well to mix.

4 Stir in the spring onion greens and basil leaves.

5 Serve hot with a spicy Thai curry.

CHEF'S TIP

As Jasmine rice is not easily available, use Basmati rice. Add around 20-25 jasmine flowers tied in a *potli* to the water in which the rice is cooked.

FRIED NOODLES WITH PRAWNS

Ingredients

350 grams egg noodles

16 (225 grams) medium prawns, peeled and deveined

3 tablespoons oil

10-12 garlic cloves, chopped

2 eggs, lightly beaten

50 grams tofu (bean curd), cut into thin strips

½ teaspoon red chilli flakes

1 cup bean sprouts

½ cup roasted peanuts, coarsely crushed

1 teaspoon sugar

1 tablespoon dark soy sauce

2 tablespoons fish sauce

2 tablespoons tamarind pulp

salt to taste

2 tablespoons chopped fresh coriander leaves

1 lemon, cut into wedges

Method

1 Bring plenty of water to a boil in a deep pan and cook the noodles till just done. Drain.

2 Heat one tablespoon of oil in a large wok; add the garlic and stir-fry till golden brown.

3 Add the prawns and cook for one or two minutes, tossing well till the prawns turn pink. Remove the prawns to a plate.

4 Heat another tablespoon of oil in the same wok; add the lightly beaten eggs and tilt the wok to coat it in a thin layer. Stir briskly to scramble the egg. Remove from the wok and add to the prawns.

5 Heat the remaining oil in the wok; add the tofu and red chilli flakes and stir-fry for a few seconds. Add the drained noodles and stir-fry for five minutes.

6 Add half the bean sprouts and half the roasted peanuts and continue to stir-fry.

7 Season with the sugar, soy sauce, fish sauce and tamarind pulp. Mix well and continue to cook until the noodles are heated through. Add salt to taste.

8 Add the prawns and scrambled eggs and mix well with the noodles.

9 Serve hot, garnished with the remaining bean sprouts and peanuts, the coriander leaves and lemon wedges.

CHICKEN RICE NOODLES

Ingredients

200 grams chicken mince (*keema*)

200 grams rice noodles

2 tablespoons oil

2-3 garlic cloves, crushed

4-5 white peppercorns, crushed

4 tablespoons chopped fresh coriander leaves

1 fresh red chilli, seeded and sliced lengthways

1 cup bean sprouts

4-5 spring onions, chopped

2 tablespoons light soy sauce

2 tablespoons fish sauce

2 tablespoons sweet chilli sauce

1 tablespoon brown sugar

2 tablespoons rice vinegar

salt to taste

2 tablespoons roasted peanuts, crushed

Method

1. Place the rice noodles in a large bowl, cover with boiling water and soak for ten minutes. Drain.
2. Heat the oil in a wok and add garlic and crushed white peppercorns. Pound half the coriander leaves to a paste with a mortar and pestle. Add to the wok and continue to stir-fry till fragrant.
3. Add the chicken mince and sauté for three to four minutes, or until lightly browned.
4. Add the red chilli and stir-fry for one minute. Add the bean sprouts and spring onions one after the other, stir-frying for a few seconds after each addition.
5. Snip the noodles into two-inch lengths with a pair of scissors. Add to the wok and toss well to mix. Add the soy sauce, fish sauce, sweet chilli sauce, brown sugar, rice vinegar and salt and toss well till heated through.
6. Transfer to a platter and sprinkle generously with the remaining coriander leaves and crushed peanuts.
7. Serve immediately.

CURRIED CHICKEN RICE

Ingredients

500 grams boneless chicken, cut into 1-inch cubes

1 cup Basmati rice, soaked and drained

3 tablespoons oil

4 garlic cloves, chopped

½ teaspoon *garam masala* powder

1 teaspoon light soy sauce

1 tablespoon chilli sauce

salt to taste

4½ cups Chicken Stock (*page* 22)

2 tablespoons chopped fresh coriander leaves

Method

1 Heat the oil in a wok; add the garlic and sauté till golden brown. Add the chicken cubes and toss well over high heat till browned on all sides.

2 Add the *garam masala* powder, soy sauce and chilli sauce and toss well to coat the chicken cubes with the sauces.

3 Add the drained rice and salt to taste. Pour in the chicken stock, stir once and bring to a boil.

4 Lower heat, cover the wok with a tight-fitting lid and simmer for ten minutes, or until the rice is cooked.

5 Remove from heat and leave to stand, covered, for ten minutes.

6 Gently mix the rice with two forks and transfer to a serving dish.

7 Serve hot, garnished with coriander leaves.

NOODLES AND VEGETABLES IN COCONUT SAUCE

Ingredients

150 grams egg noodles

1 medium zucchini, thickly sliced

½ Chinese cabbage, thickly shredded

2 carrots, thickly sliced

½ head of broccoli, cut into medium florets

1 cup Coconut Milk (*page 68*)

2 tablespoons oil

1 lemon grass stalk, chopped

1 tablespoon Red Curry Paste (*page 103*)

7-8 garlic cloves, sliced

1 medium onion, thickly sliced

2 cups Vegetable Stock (*page 17*)

salt to taste

white pepper powder to taste

2 tablespoons light soy sauce

3 tablespoons chopped fresh coriander leaves

Method

1. Heat the oil in a large wok; add the lemon grass and red curry paste and stir-fry for a few seconds.
2. Add the garlic and onion and cook over medium heat, stirring occasionally, for about five to ten minutes, or until the onion softens.
3. Add the zucchini, Chinese cabbage and carrots and mix well.
4. Lower heat and cook gently, stirring occasionally, for another five minutes.
5. Increase the heat to medium, stir in the coconut milk, vegetable stock, salt and white pepper powder and bring the mixture to a boil.
6. Add the broccoli and noodles, lower heat and simmer for another five minutes.
7. Stir in the soy sauce and coriander leaves and serve hot.

CHIANG MAI NOODLES

Ingredients

100 grams rice noodles, boiled and drained

500 grams chicken thigh meat, cut into ½-inch cubes

1 cup thick Coconut Milk (*page 68*)

2-3 garlic cloves, crushed

4-5 white peppercorns, crushed

2 tablespoons chopped fresh coriander leaves

1 teaspoon Red Curry Paste (*page 103*)

2 tablespoons dark soy sauce

2 red capsicums, chopped

2½ cups Chicken Stock (*page 22*)

salt to taste

1½ tablespoons cornflour

Garnish

100 grams rice noodles, fried

2 garlic cloves, fried and chopped

2 tablespoons chopped fresh coriander leaves

2 lemons, cut into wedges

Method

1. Pour the coconut milk into a large wok and bring to a boil over medium heat. Continue to boil for ten minutes, stirring continuously, until the milk separates and an oily layer appears on the surface.
2. Add the garlic, white peppercorns, coriander leaves and red curry paste. Cook, stirring continuously, for a few seconds, until fragrant.
3. Add the chicken cubes and toss over high heat until glossy.
4. Add the soy sauce and red capsicums and stir-fry for three or four minutes.
5. Pour in the stock and bring to a boil. Lower heat and simmer for ten to fifteen minutes, or until the chicken is cooked. Add salt to taste.
6. Add the cornflour mixed with half a cup of water and cook for two minutes.
7. Place the boiled rice noodles into warmed individual serving bowls. Ladle portions of chicken over the noodles and top with the fried noodles, fried garlic and coriander leaves.
8. Serve hot with lemon wedges.

APPLE AND BANANA FRITTERS

Mok Si Kao

Ingredients

3 medium apples
3 medium bananas
¾ cup brown sugar
1 cup rice flour
1 egg, beaten
2 cups desiccated coconut
2 teaspoons baking powder
a pinch of salt
oil for deep-frying

Method

1. Gently heat the brown sugar and three cups of water in a pan, stirring continuously, until the sugar dissolves. Bring to a boil and cook for another two or three minutes until slightly reduced and syrupy. Remove from heat and set aside to cool.
2. In a large bowl, mix together the rice flour, beaten egg, desiccated coconut, baking powder and salt; beat well to make a smooth paste.
3. Pour in the cooled syrup and beat to make a smooth batter. Set aside for twenty minutes.

4 Core the apples and cut into rings. Peel and slice the bananas diagonally.

5 Add apples and bananas to the batter.

6 Heat the oil in a wok or a frying pan; drop the pieces of fruit, generously covered with batter, the hot oil. Fry until golden brown on both sides, turning once.

7 Drain on absorbent paper and serve at once.

CHEF'S TIP

Use ripe apples and almost ripe bananas for a better taste and texture.

COCONUT PANCAKES

Kan Um Kluk

Ingredients

2 cups Coconut Milk (*page 68*)

½ cup rice flour

3 eggs, whisked

½ cup sugar

100 grams desiccated coconut

salt to taste

oil for deep-frying

To Serve

1 cup grated fresh coconut

assorted fresh fruit, chopped

Method

1 Place the coconut milk, rice flour, eggs and sugar in a large bowl and beat for five minutes. Fold desiccated coconut into the batter. Add a pinch of salt and beat well. Leave to stand for at least twenty minutes.

2 Grease a six-inch frying pan lightly by rubbing an oiled piece of muslin or paper towel over it. Heat the pan and pour a little batter into it; tilt the pan to swirl it around and coat the base in a thin layer.

3 Cook over medium heat until set and flecked with brown spots on the underside. Flip over and cook the other side. Roll up and slide onto a plate.

4 Cook the remaining pancakes in the same way and keep warm.

5 Serve the warm pancakes, topped with grated coconut and chopped fresh fruit.

COCONUT CUSTARD

Ingredients

1½ cups Coconut Milk (*page 68*)

4 eggs

5 tablespoons brown sugar

1 teaspoon vanilla essence

icing sugar, to decorate

Method

1 Preheat the oven to 150°C.

2 Whisk the eggs and sugar in a bowl until fluffy.

3 Add the coconut milk and vanilla essence and continue to whisk till well blended.

4 Strain the mixture and pour into four individual ramekins (small individual moulds).

5 Pour some water into a baking tray, place the moulds in the tray and cover with greaseproof paper so that a crust does not form on top. Pierce the greaseproof paper at intervals to allow the steam to escape.

6 Place the tray in the oven and bake for forty to forty-five minutes. Remove from the oven and leave to cool in the moulds.

7 Turn out onto dessert plates, sprinkle generously with icing sugar and serve.

FRIED PINEAPPLE

Ingredients

1 pineapple
1 tablespoon desiccated coconut
3 tablespoons butter
4 tablespoons brown sugar
4 tablespoons lemon juice
2 cups full cream yogurt, whisked
8 lemon slices

Method

1 Peel and core the pineapple and cut lengthways into half-inch thick wedges.

2 Dry-roast the desiccated coconut in a wok till lightly browned. Remove from heat and set aside.

3 Melt butter in a large heavy wok; add the pineapple wedges and cook over medium heat for one or two minutes on each side, or until pale gold.

4 Sprinkle brown sugar and lemon juice over the pineapple. Cook, stirring continuously, until the sugar dissolves completely.

5 Transfer the pineapple to individual bowls; sprinkle with roasted coconut and serve, topped with whisked yogurt and lemon slices.

COCONUT AND LEMON GRASS ICE CREAM

Ingredients

4-5 lemon grass stalks, crushed

1 cup Coconut Milk (*page 68*)

1 cup milk

3 tablespoons cornflour

½ cup sugar

¼ teaspoon salt

2 tablespoons grated fresh coconut

2 egg whites

½ cup fresh cream

1 teaspoon grated lemon rind

Method

1. Mix together the coconut milk and half the milk in a saucepan. Add the lemon grass and simmer for five minutes.
2. Mix the cornflour with the remaining milk and add the sugar and salt. Add to the coconut milk mixture and cook over low heat, stirring continuously, to make a thick custard.

3 Stir in the grated coconut, remove from heat and set aside to cool.

4 Pour the cooled custard into a bowl with a tight-fitting lid and place in the freezer until half-frozen.

5 Beat the egg whites until they form soft peaks. Whisk the cream.

6 Transfer the coconut mixture to a clean bowl. Fold in the egg whites and mix until smooth. Gently stir in the lemon rind and fold in the beaten cream.

7 Return the mixture to the freezer and freeze for three hours. Remove from the freezer and beat again till smooth.

8 Return to the freezer and freeze till firm. Serve in scoops.

TOFFEE APPLES

Ingredients

4 medium apples

4 tablespoons cornflour

1 cup refined flour (*maida*)

½ teaspoon baking powder

oil for deep-frying

1 tablespoon butter

½ cup sugar

1 tablespoon toasted sesame seeds

Method

1 Peel, core and cut the apples into quarters, and cut each quarter lengthways in half. Coat apple segments thoroughly in two tablespoons of cornflour, shaking off the excess cornflour

2 Sift together the refined flour, remaining cornflour and baking powder into a bowl. Gradually stir in one-and-a-quarter cups of water to make a smooth batter.

3 Heat the oil in a wok; dip the apple segments into the batter and deep-fry for about one minute, or until golden brown, turning occasionally. Drain on absorbent paper and keep warm.

4 Heat the butter in a pan with two tablespoons of water and sugar. Cook till the sugar melts and turns a light golden brown.

5 Remove from heat and dip the fried apple segments into the hot caramel. Sprinkle the toasted sesame seeds on top and dip in iced water to harden the crust. Remove immediately and serve.

CHEF'S TIP

You can toffee any other fruit such as bananas or lychees.

MASSAMAN CURRY PASTE

Ingredients

4 spring onions, finely chopped

12 garlic cloves, chopped

1 inch galangal

1 lemon grass stalk, chopped

2 cloves

1 tablespoon coriander seeds

1 teaspoon cumin seeds

5 black peppercorns

3 dried red chillies, soaked and chopped

1 teaspoon salt

1 teaspoon shrimp paste (optional)

Method

1. Cook the spring onions, garlic, galangal, lemon grass, cloves, coriander seeds and cumin seeds in a wok over low heat for about five minutes. Grind to a paste.
2. Add the peppercorns, red chillies and salt and grind again.
3. Add the shrimp paste and grind again.

Makes half a cup of curry paste.

GREEN CURRY PASTE

Ingredients

10 green chillies

3 shallots

9 garlic cloves

1 inch galangal

3 inch lemon grass stalk

¼ teaspoon grated lemon rind

a small bunch of coriander roots

2 teaspoons coriander seeds

2 teaspoons cumin seeds

salt to taste

Method

Grind all the ingredients to a smooth paste.

Makes half a cup of curry paste.

RED CURRY PASTE

Ingredients

10 dried long red chillies, seeded, soaked and drained

a large pinch of salt

1½ tablespoons chopped galangal

3 tablespoons chopped lemon grass

2 teaspoons grated kaffir lime rind

1 tablespoon chopped fresh coriander roots

1 tablespoon chopped red shallots

2 tablespoons chopped garlic

Method

Pound the ingredients, adding them one by one, with a pestle and mortar, to a smooth paste. Alternatively grind all the ingredients together in a grinder till smooth.

Makes half a cup of curry paste.

Books by Sanjeev Kapoor

Paperback

Title	MRP Rs.
Monsoon Medley!	99
Chill Out!	99
Mango Masti	99
Tawa-Handi Recipes	99
Sunday Specials	99
Simple Home Baking	99
Chai-Nashta	99
Mirch Mazaa	99
Sweet Temptations	95
Dal-Roti	99
Desi Sabziyan	99
Pickles, Chutneys 'n' More	99
Say Cheese!	95
Mushroom Mania	99
Noodles and Pasta	95
Makai Magic	99
Eggs	99
Desi Aloo	95
Dahi	99
Rice, Biryani and Pulao	99
Vegetarian Rice, Biryani and Pulao	99
Kadai Cooking	95
Pressure Cooking	95
No-Oil Recipes	99
No-Oil Vegetarian Recipes	99
Street Food	95
Desi Mutton	95
Thai Cooking	99
Paneer	99
Italian Cooking	95
Drinks and Mocktails	95
Vegetarian Breakfasts	99
Salads	99
Non-Vegetarian Recipes From Around The World	99
Vegetarian Recipes From Around The World	99
Seafood	99
Chicken Recipes	99
Punjabi	95
Chinese Non-Vegetarian Cooking	95
Chinese Vegetarian Cooking	99
Microwave Desi Cooking	99
Sweet Encounters	95
Soups, Salads and Sandwiches	99
Vegetarian Snacks and Starters	99
Non-Vegetarian Snacks and Starters	99

Hardbound

Title	MRP Rs.
Dakshin Delights	295
Marwari Vegetarian Cooking	295
Tandoori Cooking @ Home	250
Flavours of the Orient	250
Wrap 'N' Roll	285
TV Dinners	275
Party Cooking	275
Chaat	250
Dal and Kadhi	250
Royal Hyderabadi Cooking	250
Cakes and Bakes	295
No-Oil Vegetarian Cooking	275
No-Oil Cooking	29
Konkan Cookbook	27
Simply Indian	27
Best of Chinese Cooking	27
Microwave Cooking Made Easy	29
Khazana of Healthy Tasty Recipes	25
Any Time Temptations	22
Low Calorie Vegetarian Cookbook	25
Khana Khazana: Celebration of Indian Cookery	29
Khazana of Indian Vegetarian Recipes	27
Khazana of Indian Recipes	29

New Releases

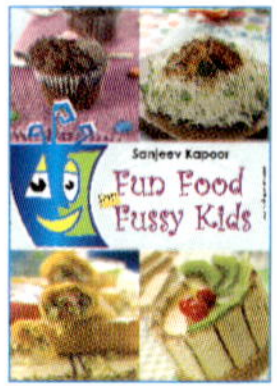

Fun Food for Fussy Kids
MRP Rs. 295/-

Simply Stylish Entertaining at Home
MRP Rs. 395/-

Healthy Tasty Recipes
MRP Rs. 99/-

Monsoon Medley!
MRP Rs. 99/-

Buy Online from www.sanjeevkapoor.com